My First Book about Horses

Amazing Animal Books
Children's Picture Books
By Molly Davidson

Mendon Cottage Books

JD-Biz Publishing

Read More Amazing Animal Books

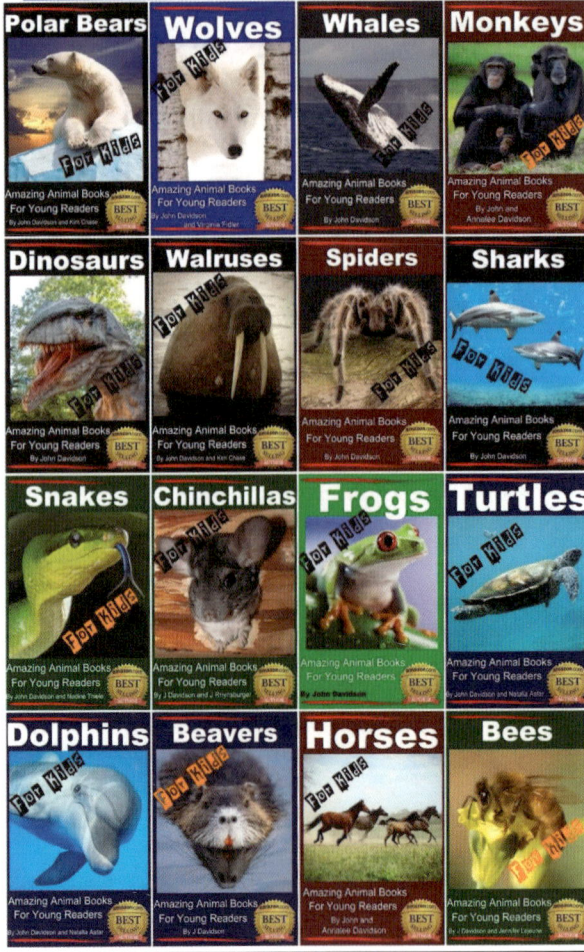

http://AmazingAnimalBooks.com

Download Free Books!

http://MendonCottageBooks.com

Table of Contents

Facts about Horses

Let's read about one of the strongest animals we know, the horse.

How Horses Are Born

A mother horse will keep her baby inside for 11 months, before it is born.

Baby horses are born with their front feet coming out first, then its nose.

A baby boy horse is called a colt, and a baby girl is called a filly.

Popular Terms for Horses

Horse lovers often use terms, when talking about their horses, here are a few:

1. Aged - this is what you call a horse that is more than nine years old.

2. Backyard horse - this horse that does not live in a barn, it lives with its owner or master.

3. Dam - this is what you call the mother of the horse.

4. Foal- this is a baby horse that is still under its mother's care.

5. Mare - this is what you call a girl horse that is already more than four years old.

6. Stallion - this means a boy horse that is already more than four years old.

How Old Does a Horse or Pony Get?

Horses usually live up to 30 years, but some live to be 40 years old.

To figure out the age of a horse, a vet will look at their teeth.

A Horses Speed

The slowest speed is called walk, then a little faster is called a trot.

The fastest speed of a horse is their gallop, where they can run between 25 - 30 miles per hour.

Another speed is in between a trot and a gallop is a speed called a canter.

Breeds of Horses

There are many different breeds of horses and they each have their own special job.

There are some horses that are great at pulling heavy objects while other horses are really good at racing.

There are many differences between the breeds of horses around today, including ears, shoulders, legs, height, and weight.

Some horses are full grown at only two feet high, like the miniature horse, and others can be five feet tall at their shoulders, which is where horses are measured from.

If you have a horse for a pet, make sure you learn as much as you can about what breed it is so you can help care for it.

Thoroughbred Horses

The thoroughbred horses are the type of horses that are well known for their use in horse racing.

They also are great for fox hunting, show jumping, dressage, and training.

These horses originated in England around the 17th and 18th century.

They were sent to other places like North America, Europe, Australia, South America, and Japan.

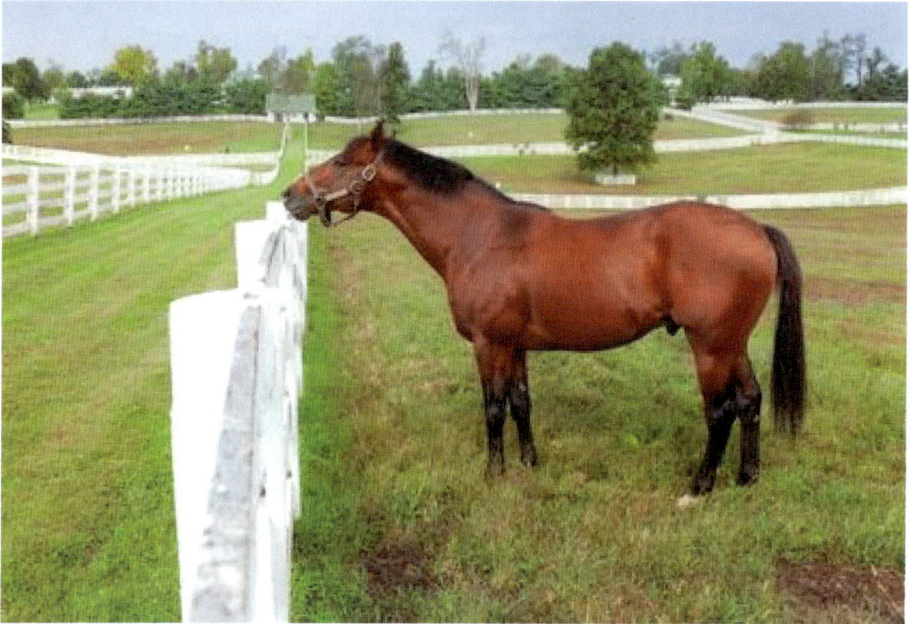

Today there are lots of them spread all over the world and about 118,000 new babies are born every year.

They have long legs and their back legs are very muscular.

The common colors of a thoroughbred are both light and dark bay (brown), black, and some are gray.

Since thoroughbreds are race horses and have to perform at high speeds, many accidents occur.

Barrel Horses

These are horses used for barrel racing. This is a sport in rodeo, where a rider must guide their horse around three barrels, as fast as possible.

Barrel horses were first used in the state of Texas for racing, around 1900.

A laser timer is used in today's barrel racing to keep time.

If a horse or rider knocks over a barrel, they get a 5 second penalty added to their score.

The barrels have to be metal, and must be painted in a least two colors.

Race Horses

Racing horses is a type of sport, which has been around for a long time.

In the first Olympic Games, in 648 BC, riders raced horses, both by riding on their backs and by riding in a chariot behind the horse.

"Carrera de carros romanos" by Poniol

Wikimedia Commons

The British gave horse racing the name of the "Sport of Kings."

In track horse racing, people can bid on the horse they think will win, if they are correct, they win money.

In 2008, $115 billion was spent on horse racing bets.

Dressage Horses

In French the word dressage means training. This means grooming and training of horses for competitions.

They are trained to perform certain skills when their trainer tells them to.

There are two types of training, western and English.

Western is mainly used in the US; the saddles are wider and easier for children.

Dressage horses are the calmest of all horses.

Shire Horses

The Shire horse is well known for its enormous capacity to pulling weights.

They were very popular in the late 19th and early 20th century for farm work.

They are many different colors, like black, bay, roan, and gray.

Their hair is very fine, straight, and silky.

Shire horses are the largest and tallest of all horse breeds.

Friesian Horses

The Friesians (also known as the Frisian horse) are from the Netherlands.

They are known for their strength, endurance, and calm nature.

They are mainly black in color; they have a long, thick mane and tail, which is often wavy.

They are small but they have always been considered as the top war horse in Europe.

They are used in farming, for pulling carriages, and as dressage horses.

Miniature Horses

Miniature horses are very common in Europe and the Americas.

These horses have a black, white, or brown coat; and some of them have all three colors.

They weigh about 150 to 250 pounds and are about 2 1/2 feet tall.

Miniature horses can live around 25 to 35 years.

Miniature horses should only be rode by someone weighing less than 70 pounds.

Even though they are friendly horses, they can kick and bite.

They eat grain and hay; one square of bale will normally last around three weeks.

Mustang Horses

Mustang horses are free roaming horses found in the west of America.

Their name 'mustang 'is from a Spanish word `mustengo' which means stray horses or horses without owners. Because these horses are reckless, they are also called wild horses.

The wild horses are believed to have escaped from ranchers, Indians tribes, Spanish explorers, and settlers in America over 11,000 years ago.

Native Indians bought the horses at high prizes from the Spanish, for traveling and for food.

Passengers traveling on trains, in the early 1900's were encouraged to shoot mustangs from the train, as entertainment on their long journey.

In 1901 there were 2,300,000 mustangs, by 1950, there was only 25,000 due to people killing them.

Now there are laws protecting mustangs, so they can stay happy and healthy.

Quarter Horses

The quarter horse is the fastest horse for short distances.

They are used in racing, working cows on ranches, rodeo roping events, and as show horses.

They have strong back legs, and a muscular body.

Quarter horses can be many colors like brownish red (called chestnut), black, brown, gray, bay (tan), blue roan, and red dun.

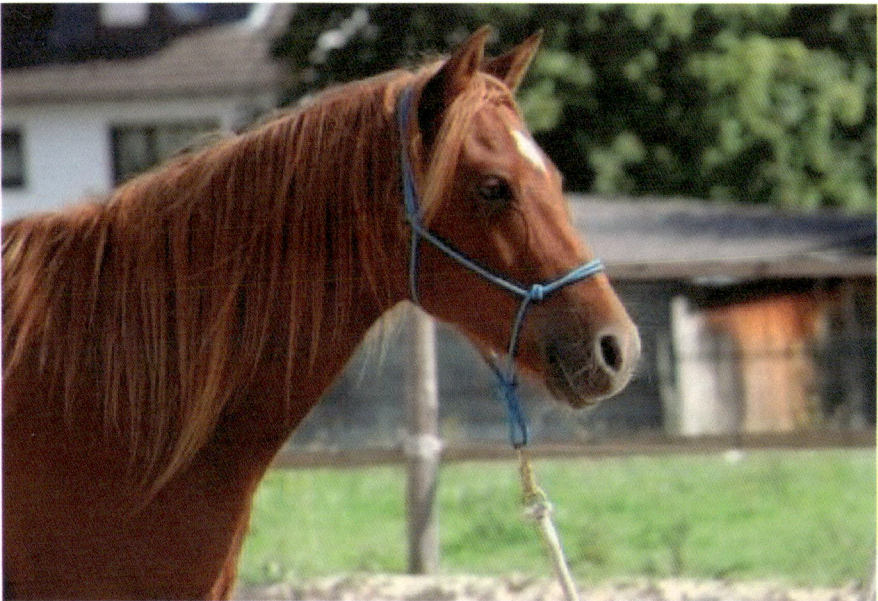

Pregnant Horses

The best time for a horse to get pregnant is in January.

After the mare is pregnant, she should be fed often. She will also need vitamins and lots of protein.

A baby horse needs to stay in their mother for 340 days, that's 11 months!

When the baby is born, it is called a foal.

Foals live off their mother's milk for the first 4 months, and then they can start eating grass like the rest of the herd.

Clydesdale Horses

Clydesdale horses are very one of a kindest horses.

They get their name from Clydesdale, Scotland, where they were bred as farm work horses.

Clydesdales are feathered tails and feet, it is not real feathers, like a bird, but they are long fluffy hairs.

These horses are also called draft horses were bred to do heavy farm work, like plowing and other farm labor.

They are very strong, on average; they can pull a car about 5 miles in an hour.

Morgan Horses

These are an American breed of horse, first owned by Justin Morgan in 1700.

This breed has great strength, and was used in wars and races.

Morgan horses are found in colors like brown, bay, black, and chestnut.

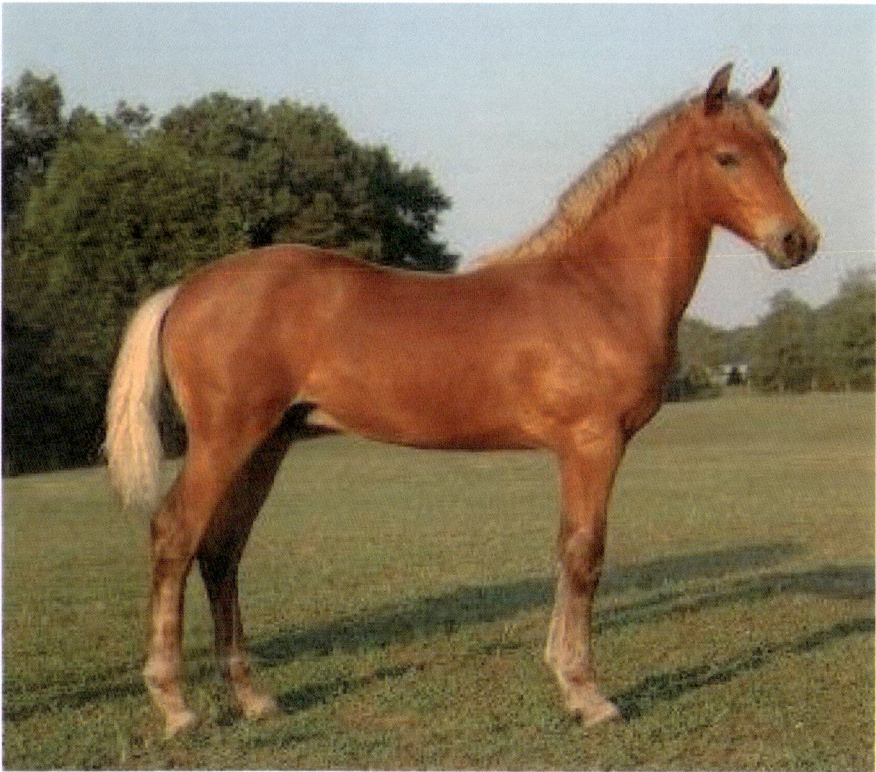

They are mostly used for pulling and driving carriages.

The Morgan horse is the official animal for the states of Massachusetts and Vermont.

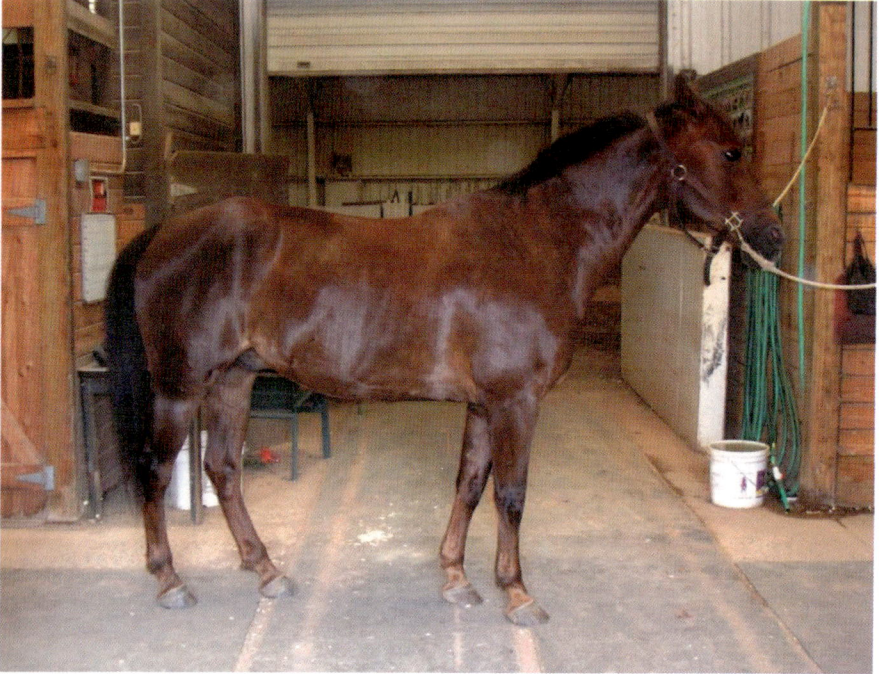

Paint Horses

This type of horse is solid white with large brown spots on it, usually on its back.

The Indians were known to ride paint horses because they believe they were free at heart.

Paint horses are also a favorite for actual paintings as well.

Riding Horses

Horses are one of the friendliest animals and are owned by many people as pets.

Before cars, horses were what most people use to get places.

Horse riding competitions used to be a huge entertainment before TV and radio.

Riding horses is still a big sport today, but many people do it more for fun now.

If you would like to ride a horse, many farms, ranches, and petting zoos, have times when you can sign up to come ride a horse.

Conclusion

Horses are amazing animals that are fun to ride and very helpful for work and play.

If you would like to learn more check out your local library or the internet, with an adults help.

Read More Amazing Animal Books

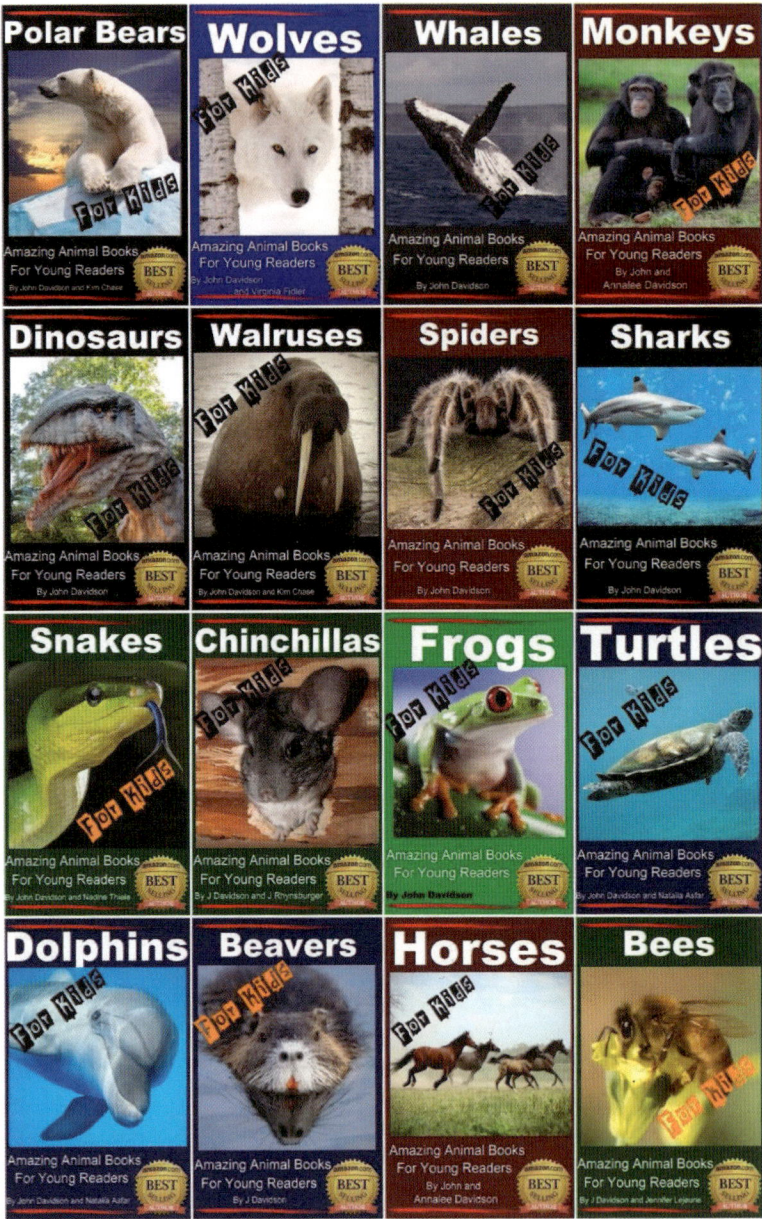

Website http://AmazingAnimalBooks.com

Horses

For Kids

Amazing Animal Books
For Young Readers

By John and
Annalee Davidson

Ponies

For Kids

Mendon Cottage Books

AmazingAnimalBooks
For Young Readers

Rachel Smith

Ten Amazing Horses

For Kids

Nature Books for Kids
JD-Biz Publishing
K. Bennett

Akhal-Teke
"The Golden Horse of the desert"
For Kids

Nature Books for Kids
JD-Biz Publishing
K. Bennett

Suffolk-Punch
"The Gentle Giant"
For Kids

Nature Books for Kids
JD-Biz Publishing
K. Bennett

Shires
"The great Horse"
For Kids

Nature Books for Kids
JD-Biz Publishing
K. Bennett

Colonial Spanish
"Horse of the Americas"
For Kids

Nature Books for Kids
JD-Biz Publishing
K. Bennett

Canadian
"The Little Iron Horse"
For Kids

Nature Books for Kids
JD-Biz Publishing
K. Bennett

Cleveland Bays
"History and Future"
Horses For Kids

Nature Books for Kids
JD-Biz Publishing
K. Bennett

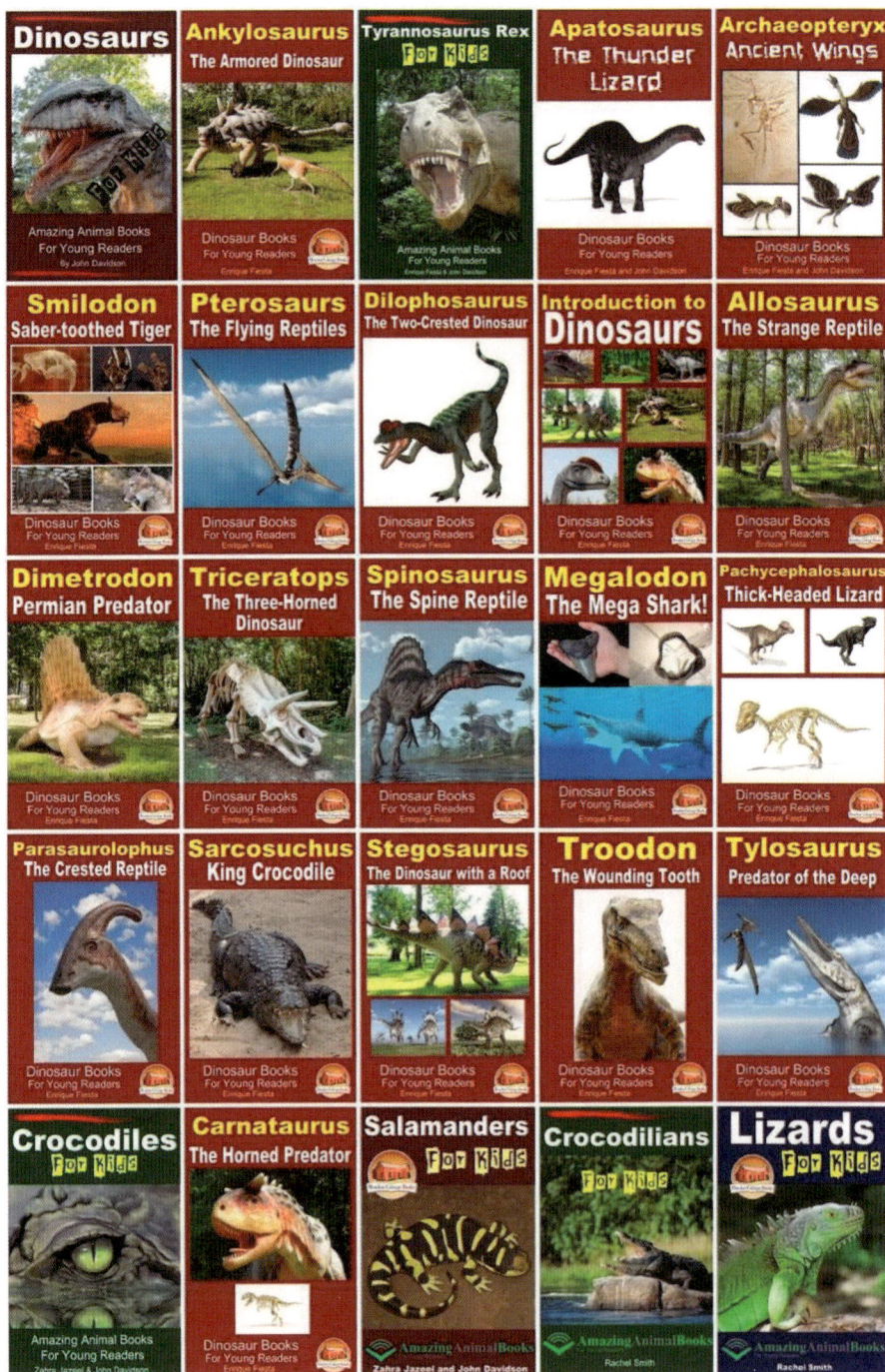

Dinosaurs
Amazing Animal Books For Young Readers
By John Davidson

Ankylosaurus
The Armored Dinosaur
Dinosaur Books For Young Readers
Enrique Fiesta

Tyrannosaurus Rex
For Kids
Amazing Animal Books For Young Readers
Enrique Fiesta & John Davidson

Apatosaurus
The Thunder Lizard
Dinosaur Books For Young Readers
Enrique Fiesta and John Davidson

Archaeopteryx
Ancient Wings
Dinosaur Books For Young Readers
Enrique Fiesta and John Davidson

Smilodon
Saber-toothed Tiger
Dinosaur Books For Young Readers
Enrique Fiesta

Pterosaurs
The Flying Reptiles
Dinosaur Books For Young Readers
Enrique Fiesta

Dilophosaurus
The Two-Crested Dinosaur
Dinosaur Books For Young Readers
Enrique Fiesta

Introduction to Dinosaurs
Dinosaur Books For Young Readers
Enrique Fiesta

Allosaurus
The Strange Reptile
Dinosaur Books For Young Readers
Enrique Fiesta

Dimetrodon
Permian Predator
Dinosaur Books For Young Readers
Enrique Fiesta

Triceratops
The Three-Horned Dinosaur
Dinosaur Books For Young Readers
Enrique Fiesta

Spinosaurus
The Spine Reptile
Dinosaur Books For Young Readers
Enrique Fiesta

Megalodon
The Mega Shark!
Dinosaur Books For Young Readers
Enrique Fiesta

Pachycephalosaurus
Thick-Headed Lizard
Dinosaur Books For Young Readers
Enrique Fiesta

Parasaurolophus
The Crested Reptile
Dinosaur Books For Young Readers
Enrique Fiesta

Sarcosuchus
King Crocodile
Dinosaur Books For Young Readers
Enrique Fiesta

Stegosaurus
The Dinosaur with a Roof
Dinosaur Books For Young Readers
Enrique Fiesta

Troodon
The Wounding Tooth
Dinosaur Books For Young Readers
Enrique Fiesta

Tylosaurus
Predator of the Deep
Dinosaur Books For Young Readers
Enrique Fiesta

Crocodiles
For Kids
Amazing Animal Books For Young Readers
Zahra Jazeel & John Davidson

Carnataurus
The Horned Predator
Dinosaur Books For Young Readers
Enrique Fiesta

Salamanders
For Kids
Amazing Animal Books
Zahra Jazeel and John Davidson

Crocodilians
For Kids
Amazing Animal Books
Rachel Smith

Lizards
For Kids
Amazing Animal Books
Rachel Smith

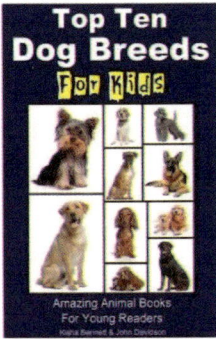

Top Ten Dog Breeds For Kids — Amazing Animal Books For Young Readers — Kisha Bennett & John Davidson

German Shepherds — Dog Books for Kids — K. Bennett

Bulldogs — Dog Books for Kids — K. Bennett

Dachshund — Dog Books for Kids — K. Bennett

Poodles — Dog Books for Kids — K. Bennett

Labrador Retrievers — Dog Books for Kids — K. Bennett

Rottweilers — Dog Books for Kids — K. Bennett

Boxers — Dog Books for Kids — K. Bennett

Golden Retrievers — Dog Books for Kids — K. Bennett

Puppies — Dog Books For Kids — Amazing Animal Books For Young Readers — By John Davidson

Beagles — Dog Books for Kids — K. Bennett

Yorkshire Terriers — Dog Books for Kids — K. Bennett

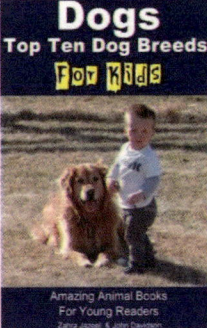

Dogs Top Ten Dog Breeds For Kids — Amazing Animal Books For Young Readers — Zahra Jazeel & John Davidson

Cats For Kids — Amazing Animal Books For Young Readers — K. Bennett & John Davidson

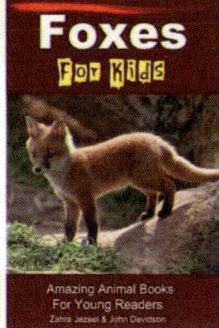

Foxes For Kids — Amazing Animal Books For Young Readers — Zahra Jazeel & John Davidson

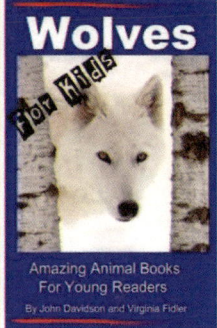

Wolves For Kids — Amazing Animal Books For Young Readers — By John Davidson and Virginia Fidler

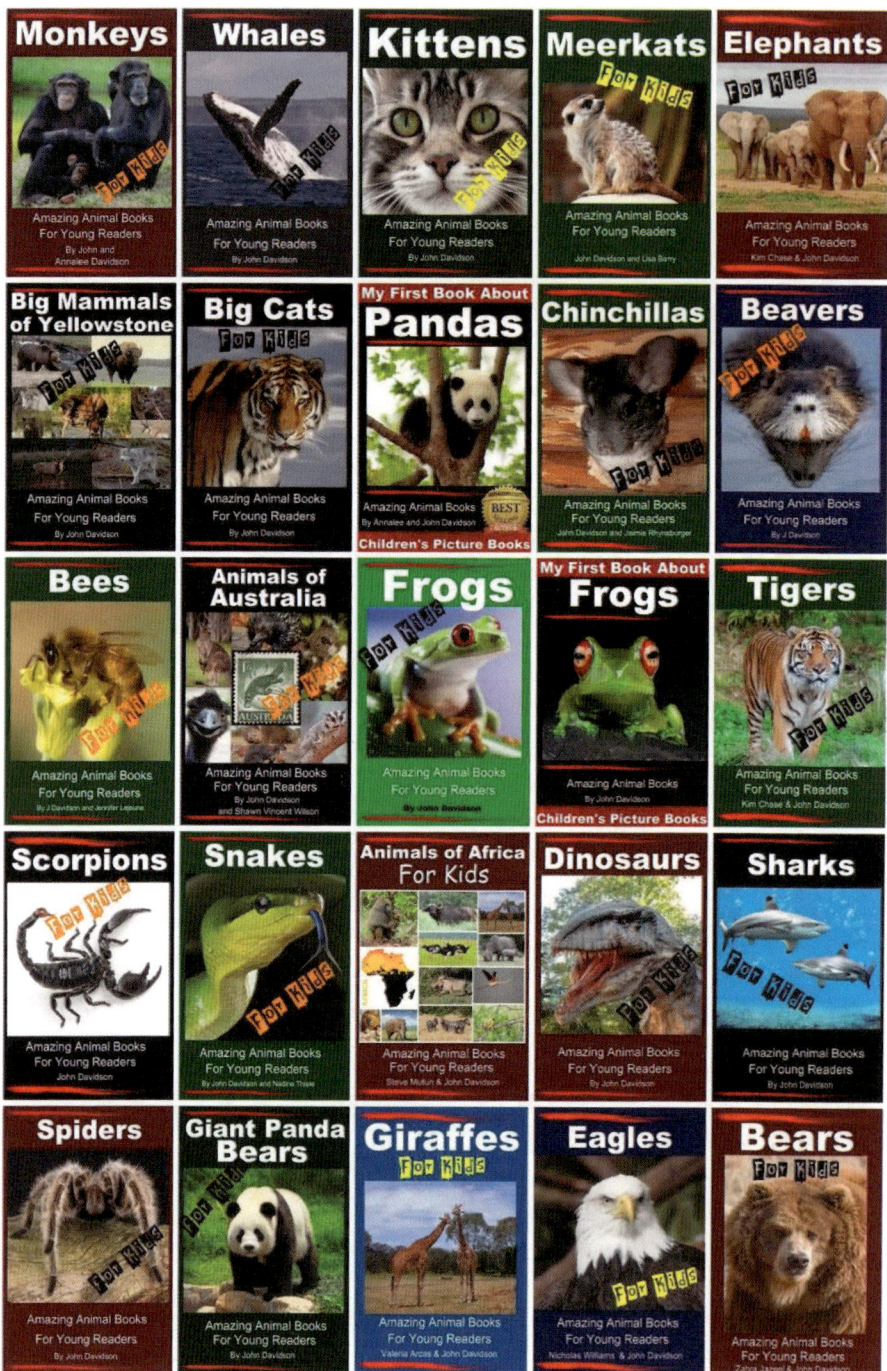

Monkeys
For Kids
Amazing Animal Books
For Young Readers
By John and Annalee Davidson

Whales
For Kids
Amazing Animal Books
For Young Readers
By John Davidson

Kittens
For Kids
Amazing Animal Books
For Young Readers
By John Davidson

Meerkats
For Kids
Amazing Animal Books
For Young Readers
John Davidson and Lisa Barry

Elephants
For Kids
Amazing Animal Books
For Young Readers
Kim Chase & John Davidson

Big Mammals of Yellowstone
For Kids
Amazing Animal Books
For Young Readers
By John Davidson

Big Cats
For Kids
Amazing Animal Books
For Young Readers
By John Davidson

My First Book About
Pandas
Amazing Animal Books
By Annalee and John Davidson
BEST
Children's Picture Books

Chinchillas
For Kids
Amazing Animal Books
For Young Readers
John Davidson and Jaimie Rhynsburger

Beavers
For Kids
Amazing Animal Books
For Young Readers
By J Davidson

Bees
For Kids
Amazing Animal Books
For Young Readers
By J Davidson and Jennifer Lepsine

Animals of Australia
For Kids
Amazing Animal Books
For Young Readers
By John Davidson and Shawn Vincent Wilson

Frogs
For Kids
Amazing Animal Books
For Young Readers
By John Davidson

My First Book About
Frogs
Amazing Animal Books
By John Davidson
Children's Picture Books

Tigers
For Kids
Amazing Animal Books
For Young Readers
Kim Chase & John Davidson

Scorpions
For Kids
Amazing Animal Books
For Young Readers
John Davidson

Snakes
For Kids
Amazing Animal Books
For Young Readers
By John Davidson and Nadine Thiele

Animals of Africa
For Kids
Amazing Animal Books
For Young Readers
Steve Mollun & John Davidson

Dinosaurs
For Kids
Amazing Animal Books
For Young Readers
By John Davidson

Sharks
For Kids
Amazing Animal Books
For Young Readers
By John Davidson

Spiders
For Kids
Amazing Animal Books
For Young Readers
By John Davidson

Giant Panda Bears
For Kids
Amazing Animal Books
For Young Readers
By John Davidson

Giraffes
For Kids
Amazing Animal Books
For Young Readers
Valeria Arcos & John Davidson

Eagles
For Kids
Amazing Animal Books
For Young Readers
Nicholas Williams & John Davidson

Bears
For Kids
Amazing Animal Books
For Young Readers
Zahra Jazeel & John Davidson

Our books are available at

1. Amazon.com
2. Barnes and Noble
3. Itunes
4. Kobo
5. Smashwords
6. Google Play Books

Download Free Books!
http://MendonCottageBooks.com

Publisher

JD-Biz Corp

P O Box 374

Mendon, Utah 84325

http://www.jd-biz.com/

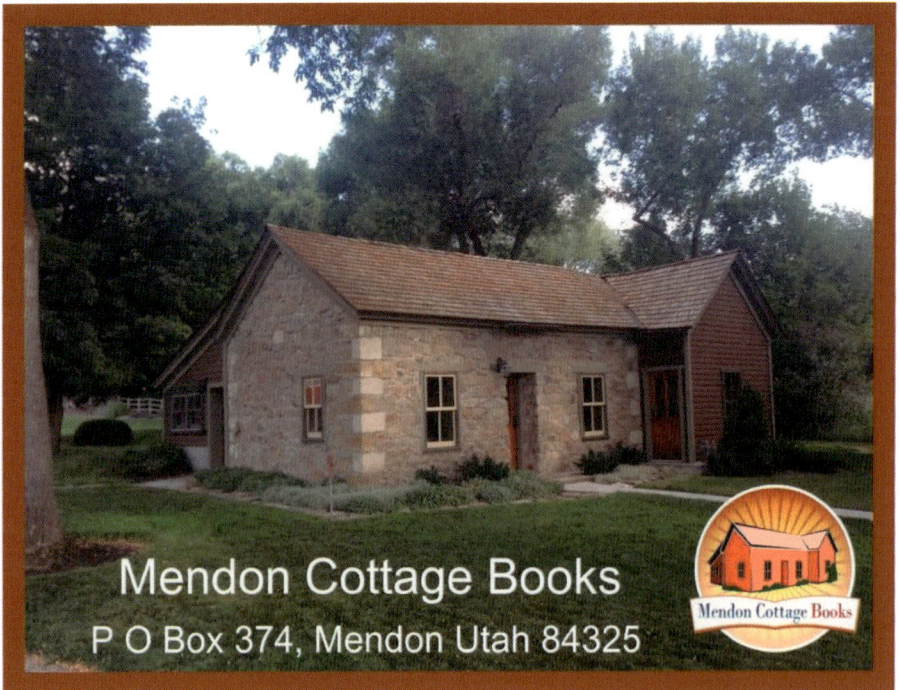

Mendon Cottage Books

P O Box 374, Mendon Utah 84325